My Oola Journey
By Jan McKee

Pastor Jim &
Patti,
Have faith ~
Live Oola
Jan

Edited by: Alisa Brackney

Published by Jan McKee 2018, All Rights Reserved

Layout and cover illustration by Jan McKee

Contents:

Dedication

First, I have to thank God and give Him all the glory for all that He has done in my life. The doors that He has opened, and the doors He has closed. The people that He has brought into my life, and the lessons He has taught me to enable me to become the person that I am. I am forever grateful, and I will live out my days sharing His good news.

Next, my loving husband, Kenny, and my children. Thank you for your love, support and grace for when I was so unOola. And my numerous friends. I am truly blessed with so many friends that I could never list them all. Please know that every one of you has touched my life in one way or another.

And finally, these two guys right here! Dr. Troy and Dr. Dave, the OolaGuru and OolaSeeker. Thank you for opening my eyes to a life of Oola. Thank you for your continued support and

encouragement throughout the years. You two are truly changing the world with your one word.....Oola! You have taught me how to balance my crazy world, how to use OolaAccelerators and stay away from OolaBlockers. Thank you or the reminder to always be grateful and have faith.

Introduction

June 6, 2017. My 50th birthday. It's time. It's time to tell my story. It's time to let others know that it's never too late to create a life of Oola.

Do you realize that a butterfly spends almost half its life as an ugly larva- trapped in a cocoon- before it develops into the beautiful butterfly? Just like the butterfly, as an ugly larva-trapped in a cocoon for nearly half of its life before it develops into a beautiful butterfly, many of us are trapped. We carry emotional baggage that weighs down our "beautiful" self! It is time to break out of the cocoon....it's time to create a balanced life that brings us to the greatness that God created us for.

Three years ago I met Dr. Dave (the OolaSeeker) and Dr. Troy (the OolaGuru). I heard them tell their story on stage and also in a class on how I too could have an Oola life. A life balanced in 7 key areas of life: Faith, Family, Friends, Finance, Fun, Fitness and Field. Since then I have been discovering my Oola life... finally, I have my wings.

This is my Oola journey.

Chapter 1- In the beginning

June 2014, I listened as Dr. Troy said these words... "You are created for greatness by God." Since 2009 I've been telling my story at Celebrate Recovery groups like Free Indeed, saying, "You are God's Masterpiece, and He doesn't make junk!" So, why don't I believe it about myself???

My Oola journey began before I was born. Mom and dad had been married for 15 years when my mom started having an affair with a police officer. After I was born and she brought me home, my grandfather vowed that he'd never love that Bastard child. When I was 6 weeks old my mom left my dad.

Things seemed to go downhill from there for the next 41 years. Sure there were good times, like the births of my four beautiful children, but my 7 key areas of life were in disarray.

I have been told for years that I should write a book. For some, my life has been unbelievable. My wish is that for those that read this, that they're able to learn from my hurts, habits, hang ups, goals, fears and failures. Honestly, I'm writing to bring closure on my larva and cocoon days, and if my words help one person push through their days, knowing that if they do, they too will get their wings and see the beautiful plan God has for them, my heart will be full.

Now, before we really get started we need to start with my squirrel prayer. You see, although I've never been clinically diagnosed with any funky letters, I do encounter many distractions in my day to day routines. During one of our morning devotions, my husband prayed, "Jesus, I come to you this morning and ask that you would wrangle Jan's squirrels. She has a lot on her plate, and needs to focus. We know that you are the ultimate squirrel wrangler, and can make her path clear from distraction." We both chuckled and a peace came over me- instead of the overwhelming anxiety that I was feeling. Since then I pray that prayer often, especially when life gets hectic, and of course I fill my diffuser with a beautiful blend of essential oils for clarity.

Chapter 2 - What is Oola?

Oola is the state of Awesomeness. When we are balanced in 7 key areas; which are Family, Friends, Faith, Fitness, Fun, Finance and Field (which is our work whether it be employment outside of the home, or a stay at home parent), we are living a life of Oola.

Think of these 7 areas as spokes on a wheel, based from our hub. I am a christian, so my hub is God, my Savior. Your hub may be something else, but we all need to be grounded in something. When our spokes are even, our tire (life), rolls smoothly, but when a spoke, or more than one spoke become shorter or longer than the other spokes, we become unbalanced, and you'll find bumps on your journey.

The trick is to acknowledge these areas of our life and examine where you are, where you want to be, and to set goals on how you're going to get there. This is my story of my journey to obtain Oola. If you'd like to learn the key steps on how to obtain your Oola life, I encourage you to purchase *"Oola, Find Balance in an Unbalanced World"* by Dave Braun and Troy Amdahl.

Here's Dr. Troy, Me, my friend, Dianna, and Dr. Dave right after I told them that I had started to write this book. These guys are always so supportive and know how to pump up our FUN!

Chapter 3 - Family

Family... I can't believe I'm starting with this F of Oola. I would like nothing more than to say my family is in perfect balance, but in reality it's one of my hardest F's to manage.

When my mom left my dad, she also left my three older siblings. They were 12, 14 and 15. From then on I was like an only child, and I envied them as I got older. Within a few months of leaving my dad, mom left me in my crib, and attempted to commit suicide. I was about 6 months old. Not sure who found me, but I was given to a wonderful couple that were friends of my dad while my mom stayed in a mental hospital. When she was released a judge thought it best for a baby to be with it's mother. Mom married her lover, the police officer, and I believe the abuse began immediately. Doctors have since confirmed that my nose has been broken and my middle sister recalls my weekend visits to dad's that I would be covered in bruises when dropped off.

The nightmares stemming from the sexual, mental and verbal abuse haunted me for years, and to be honest I believe that one never truly gets 'over' it. Eventually mom got tired of her beatings and we left Clarence when I was in second grade.

Through life I adored my father. He never treated me as anything other than his daughter. Even though there was never any paternity test, and my mother's lies were everywhere, never knowing what to believe, as far as he was concerned, I was his. Janice Marie Vincent. Period.

This picture is the most precious to me... I was only 2 months old 8/4/67, it was taken 2 weeks after my mom left my dad... A picture is worth a thousand words... but the two most important to me is love and sadness. I love you, Daddy. Thank you for never giving up on me.

And as far as my grandfather? He almost held true to his word to never love me; until I turned 20. That summer I spent a week with Pop and Grama as he was recovering from surgery. Grama and I had many long talks, and I finally understood why he treated me so differently. I grew a ton that summer, and before I went home Pop told me that he loved me.

It was that summer that I was pregnant with my first child. I was thrilled to be starting a family, and eager to be everything my mom wasn't. But my marriage was a shipwreck waiting to happen. I had only been dating my husband a few short months when I graduated from high school and turned 18 in the same

11

weekend. By Monday, mom kicked me out of the house and my soon to be husband's family had taken me in, and we were married in less than a year. I remember my older brother driving south out of town instead of to the church with me that day, saying "it's not too late, you don't have to go through with the wedding". I couldn't not go through with the wedding after all the planning, the money spent, and I couldn't disappoint others. And so, to the church I went. We had purchased a home, neighboring my in-laws, and moved in when we got home from our honeymoon.

During your Oola journey there are OolaAccelerators and OolaBlockers. An OolaAccelerator is integrity. Always do what is right, and don't be in such a hurry to reach your dreams that you compromise your values in an attempt to get there faster. *"Oola for Women"*

Two years into our marriage when our daughter was only 6 months old, I had had enough, and I had only one person to turn to...my dad. Without hesitation he and my stepmother, Janet, stepped up to the plate and welcomed me and my daughter with open arms.

That next year was amazing. While life is never perfect, I finally was able to experience what being in a normal, loving family was about. Dad taught me many things like how to change the oil and brakes on my car, and Janet taught me what it was like to have a nurturing relationship with a mother. Janet left this earth way too soon, after an 18 month battle with leukemia shortly after my youngest was born. I miss our long talks, but what I am most grateful for is that she took me to church. By age

21, I had never attended church service, until Staci and I moved in with them, and it didn't take long until I was hooked on Jesus!

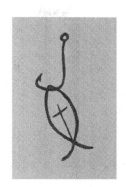

Over the next twenty years my family grew. I got remarried and we had 3 more beautiful children together. I struggled to be what I thought was the perfect mom. In the beginning of our marriage I was the breadwinner, and I thought I could do it all. Work 60 hours a week, Girl Scout leader, Sunday School teacher, help out at pre-school, swim lessons, the list went on and on.

Self sabotage is another OolaBlocker, and my biggest mountain to overcome. I was constantly fighting the voices in my head saying I wasn't good enough, and I needed to do more, and when my husband, Jim, and I started having marital problems it just escalated. His infidelity sent me over a proverbial cliff. I retreated. Feeling alone and vulnerable, I did the best I could. More OolaBlockers came into play during that time. Anger...you bet. Guilt...Yes! The one thing I never wanted for my children was for them to be a product of divorced parents, and now it looked as though I was headed for divorce #2. Fear...how on earth was I going to be a single mother of 4?

Jim and I fought hard for our marriage. Two years in counseling. Lots of talks and tears, and in the end an OolaAccelerator called humility came into play. We wanted more for our children. Jim and I were both children of divorce. And...Jim was sick. At age 15 he went into renal failure. Age 16,

13

he had his first kidney transplant, and at age 19 a second transplant.

So, here we are. Together 16 years. Jim recommitted to loving only me and our children when we got the news. His doctors confirmed that he was again in renal failure and that he could no longer work. Dialysis soon became part of our weekly routine, and I found myself having to also quit working out of the home to be a caregiver. The next 4 years were tough; physically and mentally draining with all the surgeries, the medicines, the appointments, all while still trying to be the best mom I could to four teenagers, and feeling like I was failing miserably.

In February 2009, Jim passed away. It was the darkest time of my life. My larva stage right before turning into a butterfly, but at the time I didn't know that. So many emotions flooded me. I wanted to be strong for my children. I wanted to be independent. I had convinced myself that I had no desire to be in another relationship. I didn't need a man, and I didn't want another man in my life. Have you heard the saying, "If you want to hear God laugh, tell Him YOUR plans"??? Well, I have often said that He was laughing hysterically at me as I told Him my plans for my future.... And 6 weeks after Jim's passing I "officially" met Kenny McKee.

Staci had expressed her concern that I needed someone to talk to; someone to laugh with. She suggested a dating site. No way... I wanted nothing to do with it. Remember, I didn't need or want a man. But she assured me that it would be a good thing and she had researched and found a good reputable site. After much reluctance, I completed the lengthy profile questionnaire, and they sent me one match. Really??? ONE MATCH??? Am I seriously that difficult? Ugh... I decided to reach out and give it a shot. And that's how I met, Kenny McKee. So, what do I mean by "officially" meeting Kenny McKee? What on earth could I mean by that? Well, our paths had crossed many times; the most recent only a few days before Jim had passed away. You see, Kenny owns a pawn shop, and Jim's mom had been a friend of his for years. She passed away only 9 days before Jim did. At the time of her passing she had jewelry in Kenny's shop, and Kenny would only release it if all three of her children came to sign for it at once. So, with Jim's two siblings, we went in to collect her items. I don't remember a whole lot of that day, as we were overwhelmed with the task at hand of taking care of her estate.

As Kenny and I started communicating via email, then text, we progressed quickly to a phone call. It was April 5, 2009, Kenny called me on his way home from his sister's house after celebrating his mom's birthday. I remember this call like it was yesterday. I asked him about his work. On his profile it said that he was self employed, being an entrepreneur myself, I was curious. He replied sheepishly that he owned a pawn shop. Already declaring our love for the Lord, and knowing that pawn shops sometimes get a bad rap, he wasn't sure how I would respond. Even though I had never pawned anything, I knew that pawn shops also had great deals on used items, and being a very frugal person, I'm all about that. So, I continued with "which one?", he replied with, "Music Ma..." " WHAT? You're Kenny from the Music Man???", I blurted, not even letting him finish his sentence. It was true. The man who was once a friend of my mother-in-law, a man who had sold us a gun for our son, and another time a drum set for our daughter, was the ONE match.

Love was instantly in the air, and a true OolaAccelerator. I was feeling alive again. Kenny brought out the best in me. He showed me my value within myself, that I didn't even know I had. But it was soon, too soon. And not all of my children were ready for such change. Kenny had another OolaAccelerator, and that is wisdom. He knew we needed to take things slow. So with discipline, integrity and gratitude we nurtured our relationship. These things can truly accelerate you in your Oola Life, but you need to set goals, and evaluate the steps to achieve those goals. In our case, we had to evaluate where each child was in their journey of grief over losing their father. It was hard. Every one of us was in a different state of emotion. I admit that I failed my children at times during this period of our journey. I remember being so frustrated at not being able to find clinical research about grief. What should I be feeling? Was it normal? What about my children? How are they feeling?

It's been 8 1/2 years since Jim's passing. Kenny and I have been married for 7. The children are grown and all out on their own. My dad passed away 6 months after Kenny and I got married, my siblings and children all live on the other side of the state or out of state. My mom is in a nursing home 2 hours away in a vegetative state due to advanced Alzheimer's Disease. I still struggle every day to have balance in my family, but I continue to push through. I do what I can and commit the rest to God. I strive for weekly calls to the kids, and cardmaking dates with my new mother-in-law and sister-in-law.

This is what I thought to be the end of this chapter, but God is continually working in our life. On Saturday, July 1st, I started Monique McLean's *21 Days of Prayer over your Business*. If you've been through her 21 days of prayer, you know that day 2 is *Freedom from the Past*. On Monday, day 3 of the 21 days, Kenny and I were in the same town as my mom's nursing home for work. I had not seen her in 3 years and honestly had not thought of visiting, during our time there; however, as I dropped Kenny off at the job site, God put it on my heart, "Hey, you should drive the extra mile up the road and see your mom".. And so I did. I walked in and she was laying on her bed, that is barely off the floor, as I leaned down she looked at me. I said, "Hi, Mom", and she replied, "Hi" with a smile. I was in total shock, as I was not expecting that at all. As I was sitting next to her, a nurse in the hall was talking to a nurse aid and said the word "Margaret" as to which my mom flinched. Margaret was my grandmother. My mom's mom. Then God again laid these words on my heart, "It was learned behavior". I then told mom, "I forgive you, Mom. I know that it was learned behavior from your mom, and I forgive you. I love you, and I pray that you know Jesus, Mom. I pray that you've accepted Him as your Lord and Savior, and that I will see you in Heaven with a restored body and mind." To which her smile turned sad, and a tear formed in her eye. I told her again that I loved her and left.

I think one of the hardest things in my baby steps as a christian is being still and listening to those times when something is laid on your heart, and trusting that it is God nudging you to do something that will guide you onto His plan for your life.

Fall 2012

January 2013

Aly's Wedding
June 2014

Chapter 4 - Friends

Friends... This F of Oola really threw me for a loop. We need friends. Not just acquaintances, but real friends. When I started my Oola journey and went to the website (www.oolalife.com) to take my free life balance test, I was asked to rate where I was in my area of Friends. Well, I have lots of friends. I mean, look at my Facebook... I have over 1,100 friends! But, do I really? Or are they just acquaintances? How many times do you do things with friends? Do you have lunch dates? Do you go on girl getaways? Do you talk on the phone everyday? No, no, no and no. Wow, what a wake up call.

Having friends is an important part of having an Oola life, it creates the balance that we need in life. I always struggled with having friends in school, I often refer to myself as the ugly duckling. The outsider that never fit in. Maybe it was because I was quiet, I learned at a very young age, that I was to be seen and not heard. If I spoke up when out in public, I remember getting 'the look' from mom. And so I learned that it was best to keep quiet. When I was 9, mom remarried. I liked Leo from the start. He was reserved like me. We spent most evenings at home, just the 3 of us. Sometimes playing a board game, or watching TV, but very rarely did we go to friends, and I don't ever remember friends coming to our house. With Jim Rohn's voice ringing through my head, "it's just the way it is".... I didn't know any different.

Yes, I do have friends, and I have learned to cultivate those friendships. You can't just have friends that you see occasionally, or message on facebook. You have to take time to reach out to them, sit down for coffee, and enjoy actual facetime. Friends are those that you can share mutual passions and fun, and call on when times are tough.

And then there are the 'friends' that literally suck the joy right out of your life. I know first hand that this is easier said than done, but you have got to set boundaries. For some you have to cut them right out of your life, trust me; I have been there. When I heard Dr. Dave say I would have to cut someone out of my life, I thought there was no way. I can not hurt someone like that. But what were they doing to me? I would avoid phone calls, and messages, because within minutes of being around them my sails were torn and my ship was sinking. Do you have someone like that in your friends circle? Start setting boundaries, and when possible make the cut. It's amazing how your countenance goes up when you are around positive, uplifting people who care about you. I personally am a helper. I feel that excessive need to help EVERYONE. I have finally learned that helping some people is just not possible. And when helping others, I cannot lose myself, or I'm no good to anyone.

I know that this may sound strange, but it takes discipline. I used to be very naive, now I'm just a little bit naive.... But in the earlier cocoon days, I thought everyone was honest and true to their word. I was a Senior in High School when a friend's dad talked to me about honesty and integrity. As a child, I believed what people said and did as true...doesn't everyone? You don't know what you don't know, right? It wasn't until I got older and this gentleman sat me down to have a heart to heart. I had been dating his son for about a year, and we were breaking up for the last time. Pat and I didn't talk for long, but he gave me something to really think about. "You say you don't like all the lies your mom tells, and you see where it gets her... Is that really what you want for your life?" My life drastically changed that day. I had grown up in an environment where truth and lies were so skewed, and I didn't know what I didn't know. But that day, I learned that honesty is always best, and people will like you more for it! I have to admit it wasn't always easy, and there were times when a lie would start to come out of my mouth, and I would stop and say, "I'm sorry, that's not exactly the way it was...." Humility is such an Oola Accelerator.

Always keep in mind the 3 types of friends in Oola. The close friend that you talk with daily and/or have lunch with. The numerous acquaintances that fill your social tank. And the toxic friends that you have to cut out of your life or at least set very specific boundaries with.

I find myself getting so caught up in other F's of Oola that I don't make those phone calls or lunch dates. Friends is definitely another F that I struggle to keep balanced. I believe part of it is my self worth. It's very difficult for me to see my self worth as being very high. "What do I have to bring to a friendship? I can't afford to go away for weekend getaways, or fancy shopping sprees. Why would anyone want to be my best friend? I'm nothing special. I don't know what to talk about." It has taken me many years to not feel socially awkward. I am way more comfortable standing up in front of hundreds of people speaking than I am one on one. Why do I do this??? One word… Self-sabotage!

The isolation, and abuse as a child still plays havoc in my life even decades later. I remember my first friend. Her name was Lisa. Her family moved into our neighborhood at the end of our fifth grade of school. Sure, I had kids at school that played on the playground, but no friends outside of that before then. 12. I was twelve years old before having a friend to walk home with. To ride bikes with on the weekend. 12...wow, let me let that soak in a minute.

When I was in first grade, mom had hired a babysitter to come stay with me after school until her and my step-dad got home from work. I vividly remember one day the babysitter had found some neat dress up clothes in my mom's room, and asked if I wanted to play? My mom was a wonderful seamstress, and had made costumes for her and I for a Centennial parade a few years before this. It sounded like so much fun, to dress up and play; I was so excited. And then…. mom came home early. The babysitter was fired on the spot, and from then on I got a house key put on a piece of yarn that hung around my neck every morning as I left for school. I was to go straight home and not to let anyone in. Do you realize that a couple of hours can feel like an eternity to a 6 year old? I remember watching the clock and hiding behind the floor length drapes at the front window if they were even a minute past their time that they would normally be home. Fear… fear is another oola blocker. For me, it's the fear of abandonment. Why are they late? Are those sirens? What if they were in an accident? I have to admit that I still hear those fears creep into my mind when someone I love doesn't answer their phone, or isn't home when they said they would be. I've come to realize that this is the enemy, and I cling to my hub and read His Word. I especially like Ephesians 6:12 (NLT) "For we are not fighting against flesh-and-blood enemies, but against evil rulers and authorities of the unseen world, against mighty powers in this dark world, and against evil spirits in the heavenly places." Using my hub, my God and His Word to pump up when an area starts getting low is my saving grace. It's where I go when an oola blocker comes in trying to create unbalance. That, and my essential oils. Knowing that these little bottles of goodness come from God's creation brings about such peace. Have you ever tried putting a drop of essential oil in your hands, rub your hands together, and then cup your nose and mouth and just slowly inhale? Ahhhhh.... Game changer, I tell you...game changer.

In the last couple of years, I have reconnected with friends from 20 years ago, and made new friends. It doesn't come naturally to me, but I am committed to my new life of Oola and make sure to schedule lunch dates, and talk on the phone or in person. I have found a new tribe. These friends are so incredibly dear to me, and I treasure each and everyone of them.

I love this picture! A group of us went to the Girlfriends in God Conference.
Very Oola!!!

These two amazing women, Page and Dawn, are such an inspiration to me. As part of my upline in my MML business we get to travel and help others every day.

This girl right here is my dearest and oldest friend. Lori and I are so blessed by our friendship. There was a time that life was unOola, and didn't talk for months even years, but now our friendship is stronger than ever as we both strive for our Oola Life.

Chapter 5 - Faith

"O Lord, I will honor and praise your name, for you are my God. You do such wonderful things! You planned them long ago, and now you have accomplished them." Isaiah 25:1 (NLT)

Remember in Chapter 3 how I said I had never been to church service until age 21? Well, I should have been clearer. I did not remember attending a church service until then. My mom and dad were presbyterian. They were married at the First Presbyterian Church of Lapeer, Michigan. My older 3 siblings were baptized there. My dad and my step-mom were also married there, and my grandmother was a member. So, when I started attending with my step mother, I just assumed I was also a member. In fact, no one else ever questioned it either. I ended up getting married there, and all four of our children were baptized there. It wasn't until after Jim died that I found my baptism papers and discovered that I was actually Lutheran!

I don't have many memories of Clarence's mother except that she was very religious and that she had given me a Bible when I was little. She belonged to St Paul Lutheran church of Lapeer, and was discouraged that at 13 months old I had not yet been baptized. Since neither my mom nor my step-dad were attending church, she was concerned that I wouldn't be, and so she took it upon herself to get me baptized. Kenny had attended St Paul Lutheran Church in Flint, was baptized and confirmed. He even attended their parochial school. Now he lived about 40 minutes away, and attending St Paul Lutheran Church in Millington where he is still a very active member. I ended up attending their new member classes and was confirmed at St Paul - Millington before our wedding. Isaiah 25:1 is my confirmation verse.... If you don't think God knows you before you were born, and the plans that He has for your life; think again.

When my kids were young I taught Sunday School for about 8 years. I also worked at our church as a wedding coordinator for extra income. But it's only been the last eight years that my relationship with Christ has gotten stronger and more intimate.

It has been difficult for me to balance my faith. Remember when I told you that I have a need to help everyone??? About three years ago, I closed my business and was no longer committed to a 9-5 brick and mortar job. With my new found time freedom I started committing to more and more responsibilities at church. Before I knew it I was the chairman of the Board of Social Concerns, VP of our women's group, very active in our local Ministerial Alliance, Altar Guild, coordinating our Christmas Giving Tree program, and helping coordinate lunches for a local homeless shelter. These are all wonderful programs and although I've been excited to be a part of them it has created unbalance and I'm having to reevaluate my commitment. I've come to admit that I have a control problem. In my past there has been so much that I haven't been able to control, that when I have a chance to control something, I tend to do just that... It's definitely something I'm working through, and by reevaluating my duties in the church I'm learning to let go of the control and hand jobs over to others. Seeing others take over duties you once did is actually pretty cool. You get to see God work now in their life, and give them purpose. We all need to find our purpose in life. Some things come and go for only a season, some things last a lifetime. God gives each and everyone of us talents and gifts. It's important to dig deep within yourself to research and recognize what your talent is and how you can use it to spread God's love.

In 2010 a very special young woman in my life lost her two and a half year old daughter to a horrific incident. I started an annual fundraiser to raise awareness of child abuse. After 5 events, I turned this event over to another friend of mine. At first, I felt defeated, like I was letting Lily down by not continuing to host this event, but in reality I was letting go, and handing it over and giving someone else a purpose to help spread Lily's story. That certainly is not a bad thing. I seem to have a talent for organizing events, but using that talent to get things started does not mean that I have to do them forever. Finding others who are fitted to continue the work I've started is just another way of spreading God's love. If you have a talent for fundraising, or a heart for speaking out against child abuse and would like to learn more about Lily's story, please visit www.justiceforlily.com

I feel like the best way to keep my Oola Faith in balance is to start every day in prayer. Kenny and I have done many devotionals. *"The Love Dare 365 day Couple Devotional"*, *"21 Days of Prayer for Your Business"*, *"Portals of Prayer"* and *"My Daily Bread"*. These are all great ways to start off your morning,

28

find time to spend in prayer whether as a couple or by yourself. Just quiet time with God. Giving Him time to speak into your life, and directing you onto His path for your life. Life gets busy, so you might have to think out of the box. I have sat on our bed and read as Kenny is getting ready for work, and I have taken it on the road. We have a 40 minute commute to work now, so this gives us perfect time to do a devotion with plenty of time for discussion also.

In addition to prayer time, I consciously watch my surroundings. What I'm watching and what I'm listening to. About 18 years ago, a new friend of mine introduced me to christian contemporary music and a local radio station, Smile FM. What a game changer!!! We all know that music soothes the soul, but what I have found is that this music not only soothes the soul, but heals the heart, and clears the mind. I have been in a state of mind where I felt lost or confused, and just the right song will come on the radio, letting me know that I am loved, and to trust in Jesus, for his ways are always good. That He is a good, good father that sets my soul on fire! If you have not listened to contemporary christian music I encourage you to go to YouTube and search *"Even If"* by Mercy Me, and let the words of this song just sink in. In our area, there are several great radio stations like

I KNOW

YOU'RE ABLE
AND I KNOW YOU
CAN SAVE THROUGH
THE FIRE WITH

YOUR MIGHTY HAND

BUT EVEN IF YOU
DON'T MY HOPE

IS YOU ALONE.

Smile FM, K-Love and Family Life Radio. You can search their websites to find a local station or stream online.

The same goes for what I watch on TV. Gone are the days of soap operas, with young adults hopping from bed to bed, along with marital affairs, or a show filled with language that makes my ears bleed. I found a great source of christian movies and TV shows called Pure Flix. I love that I can pick anything from here to stream onto my phone, smart tv or Roku and know that it won't be filled with nudity or language I don't want to hear. I used to be called a Prude for not wanting to watch or listen to such things. And you know what? I don't care. I'm proud that I stood up for myself, and would not cave to the peer pressure that was around me. To this day; "My radio? My rules. End of discussion."

Balancing your OolaFaith can be filled with lots of things. There are so many organizations out there that need volunteers.
Remember, Jesus said, *"Truly, I tell you, whatever you did for one of the least of these brothers and sisters of mine, you did for me." - Matthew 25:40*

Chapter 6 - Field

Field? What??? Oh... career field. Yes. Keeping with the theme of F's, our next F of Oola is Field. Whether you are a doctor, a clerk, a student or a stay at home parent this F is all about what you dedicate your life to.

I've had many different jobs. In high school I started out as an office clerk which led to office manager positions. At one time I was an office manager of a building company. That position led me to achieve my real estate license and then later my builder's license and become a Kitchen and Bath Designer. I love working with people, sales and being creative; so this seemed like the perfect job. At one point I was an office manager, working with two other women builders, and we were rocking out some beautiful homes, but integrity seemed to be an issue, and I got sucked in. I believed they would hold true to their word, and when they didn't I lost my integrity that I had worked for so hard. Good thing is that I learned quickly and when they came to me after my third daughter was born wanting to use my builder's license to continue their business, I declined to be a part of their unethical practices. I had been the breadwinner in the family. Not knowing which way to go after that, Jim and I sat down and reevaluated our finances. He had moved up in his job, and we decided that I would stay home with our girls. I did odd jobs such as bookkeeping from home, and mucking stalls. While I enjoyed being able to be more involved in school activities, I missed getting out of the house and the extra income a job brought in. That's when I discovered MLM's. Yes, Multi-level marketing. Pyramid schemes? No. Multi-level marketing. Where I actually got paid for showing someone my favorite products. I tried several. Amway, Avon, Pampered Chef, Stampin' Up! I even tried to create my own when I started making soy candles. I was at the peak of making my soy candles that were now in 5 locations across the state when Jim died. Then everything seemed to come to a halt.

I had chosen MLM because it allowed me to not only be home with my children when they were little, but then as Jim got sicker it also allowed me to be home with him to be there to take him to doctor appointments and dialysis, to stay home on the days that he couldn't make it to the bathroom without help, or open a bottle of water to take his medicine. But now he was gone. My children were growing and in school full time. So there I sat. In the living room. In silence. Staring at his chair that he died in. I was lost. My purpose was gone. I drifted into a deep depression for a few weeks, only looking forward to after school when the kids got home. I thank God for my pastor and his wife who helped me snap out of that wretched daily cycle, and showed me hope for a future. I quickly looked into college courses, and was enrolled in Spring semester. A nurse! That's what I'll be. After all, I've been taking care of Jim for the last four years, this must be my calling. Or not.... college is hard. Especially when you haven't been in school for 20+ years, you're raising 3 teenagers, and financially and emotionally stressed. Ugh! I stuck it out for a little bit. I think the pivotal moment for me was May 18th. I sat down in my Biology class ready to take an exam, when I went to put the date on my paper... May 18, 2009. Wait...what? "Today is May 18th?", I asked the girl sitting next to me. Then it hit me. What was I doing? How could I think that I could do all of this when I haven't even recovered from Jim's death. Yes, I had met a wonderful man who was treating me like a queen. But today... I forgot that today would have been my 18th wedding anniversary. No one prepares you for death, and the grieving process. Sometimes it just comes up and slaps you upside the head without warning. I left the room in tears.

So, what do you do when you fall off a horse? Try, and try again. I started attending a group called Free Indeed. They met weekly and helped others work through hurts, habits and hangups. Going to these meetings where I got to worship the Lord, and talk through my feelings helped me immensely. I highly recommend anyone going through hard times, whether it's grief, addiction or abuse, to seek out a christian based group such as this. Celebrate Recovery is a Christ centered recovery program with meetings all across the country. You can go to www.celebraterecovery.com to find a meeting near you.

I took time off from finding a career, and concentrated on me. It had been a long time since I had done that. It wasn't easy. Moms seem to have guilt when they try and do something for themselves. I especially struggled with this. I had a friend that owned a scrapbook store. I worked for her when she needed help, and she let me put my candles in her store to sell. I taught classes on card making and held scrapbooking events. It was during this time that Kenny and I were falling in love, and I knew that I could take the time to figure out what I now wanted to be when I grew up, lol. As we were getting closer to our wedding, I was feeling more anxious about getting back to work. I was missing working with people, and the purpose that a job gives me. Not that being a mom isn't a job, but my relationship with my children at this time was strained and I needed to feel needed. Kenny was working with his dad and his brother at their pawn shop, and I was bored.

Two months after we were married I got a phone call from a friend letting me know of a fabulous opportunity to buy a scrapbook store that was located only 12 miles from my new home. I was ecstatic! The thought of owning my own store, doing something I loved was just what the doctor ordered! Or so I thought…. Yes, I loved having my own store, but it was located within a mall with very strict regulations on when I had to be open. It had to be open 7 days a week, 9am until 6pm. Needless to say my OolaField went from one end of the spectrum to the other. I was so out of balance, it didn't take long for things to start falling apart. I had a new husband that I hardly got to see, let alone the new grandson that was born only a month before I bought the store. Then my father passed away, then my father-in-law, and then 13 months after my father passed away, my step-father passed away. I was done. Stick a fork in me and flip me over. I. Am. Done. I had mounds of bills, and a lease to fulfill. Through prayer and many conversations, Kenny and I found a smaller location outside of the mall, closer to our home; and we decided to give it a shot.

It was here that I see God was preparing us for our future. Kenny is a jeweler, and was only working part time at his pawn shop. He asked me about combining both of our businesses in our new location. We began working together, and tackling the debt I had incurred. We worked really well together, and he taught me some of his trade. Soon I was cleaning jewelry, learning how to buy gold, and taking measurements for sizing rings. And he would run the register while I taught classes. Before too long I had made my last payment on the old lease, and the proverbial noose that was around my neck was loosened.

But then I started having some health issues, and from everything I had seen Jim go through I did not want to start taking medications. I knew that it too often led down a path of one medication leading to another, and yet another. It was then that I was introduced to essential oils. I found instant relief and was sold. I wanted them all! I got my first order, and was so impressed and excited on how well they were working and how great I was feeling, that I couldn't help but tell my friends. And lucky for me this company that I had found to buy my essential oils from was a MLM. Sweet!!!! I started earning money right away, and before I knew it I had earned a Mediterranean Cruise out of Venice, Italy, and ranked up in the company. I had purpose! Yes, teaching classes at my little scrapbook store was fulfilling, it was very therapeutic, but this was over the top. I was really helping people. I was giving them hope, when they thought there was none. I was seeing people's lives being changed one drop at a time.

It was the Friday before Mother's Day 2014. I went with my mother-in-law and sister-in-law to a scrapbooking convention. We had a fabulous time. I got to talk with people, and see the new product, and even make a few items. I hadn't had that much fun in a long time. I went home and was showing Kenny my treasures, and before I knew it the words were coming out of my mouth. "What do you think about me closing the store?"

"WHAT?? What did you just say? Seriously? You're thinking about closing? I thought we'd grow old on that corner of our little town."- he replied. I really couldn't believe I had said it either, but it was that day that I realized how much I was missing. We now had 4 grandchildren, and our youngest daughter was getting married the following month. I wanted to travel, I wanted to go and teach people how to use these beautiful bottles of goodness from God. And I wanted to scrapbook and make cards, not for classes that no one showed up for, but for me. The industry had changed. The big box stores were drowning out the little guys with their discounts and big chain buying power. It was draining to have someone come in my door wanting me to show them how to use something that they bought online with a great coupon. And so, we went to dinner on Sunday with the family, and announced we were closing.

On Monday we started the store closing sales, and by the end of the month, we were moved out and headed to Florida for our daughter's wedding. I started rocking the business of our MLM as soon as we got back. I set up an office at home, and had lots of ideas ready to implement. I was traveling everywhere and anywhere someone wanted to learn about essential oils. There's a couple of Oolablockers that I don't think I've mentioned.... Laziness and Focus. I was doing really well and somehow, before I knew it I was losing focus, and getting lazy. It was really hard for me to admit for a long time. I would find myself watching TV instead of in my office making calls, I would start a project and not finish it. Next thing I knew, my business was at a standstill.

I had gotten way out of balance. I wasn't getting out and meeting new people to tell them how essential oils could change their lives. I buried myself in volunteer positions at church. My Faith spoke on my Oola wheel had gotten very long, while my Field spoke grew shorter. It's so important to continually evaluate your 'spokes' of Oola. They can get out of balance quickly and before you know it, you've strayed off from your Oola Path.

In November 2015, my brother-in-law approached Kenny about turning the pawn shop over to him. Steve realized that the economy was not what it used to be and the shop was struggling to provide for two families. While Kenny and I were nervous about what that would look like for us, we took Steve up on his offer and bought him out. The first year was a struggle to just figure things out. Yes, Kenny had worked at this pawn shop since his dad opened it 45 years ago, but now everything rested on his shoulders. With his dad and brother gone, Kenny was able to take hold and steer this ship in the direction of a vision he had had for years. I started working a day or two a week at the shop helping out; the customers quickly acknowledged my presence, and I was connecting with people again. Remember- how I mentioned that back in January of 2012 when I moved my scrapbooking store to our small town, and Kenny came in and we started working along side of each other, I saw how God was preparing us for our future? Well, now here we are, working side by side again. Kenny had shown me enough back then about buying gold, and working with jewelry that I felt confident when he asked me to come alongside and work with him at the pawn shop. He shared that his vision was bigger than just the pawn shop the way it had been for the last 25 years. He wanted to remodel, and in the plans for that remodel, he wanted to include a case to display our essential oils. You see, Music Man Pawn Shop is not your ordinary pawn shop. Kenny has always called himself God's Pawnbroker. He has tattoos on his forearms. One is Jeremiah 29:11 "For I know the plans I have for you," declares the Lord, "plans to prosper you and not to harm you, plans to give you hope and a future." Another one is Romans 6:23 "For the wages of sin is death, but the gift of God is eternal life in Christ Jesus our Lord." These tattoos create a lot of conversation. The majority of our customers are going through a difficult time. They come in needing money, but many times leaving with oh so much more. We have prayed with people, given them direction towards organizations that could help them through a situation, or sometimes it was just a smile showing them that someone cares. Bringing in our essential oils gives us just one more avenue to connect with people in need.

So, here we are... Fall 2017. The remodel is almost complete. Kenny's vision for the remodel is already proving itself to be successful. He even set up a corner of the office for me to have a desk where I can run my essential oil business while at the pawn shop. We have prayed over this transformation of our businesses for months. We went through Monique's 21 *Days of Prayer for Your Business*. The sky's the limit, and we are so excited to see God's plan play out in this next step of our journey.

Chapter 7 - Finance

Finance... yuck! Yuck? Why do I feel that way? I love numbers. At one time during my Oola Journey I thought I wanted to be an Accountant. That's right. I even received a scholarship for a business college right out of high school. But if you'll recall my life drastically changed the Monday after graduation. Loving to work with numbers and balance checkbooks doesn't make your Oola Finance strong. Making sound financial decisions is what makes your F of Finance balanced.... And that, my friends, is what I lacked along my Oola Journey.

I was never given an allowance when I was younger. As I became a teenager and visiting dad on the weekend, I can remember him slipping me twenty dollars so I had pocket money to go to McDonald's with my friends. But that was the only experience I had with money- until I got my first job at age 16. By this time, I now had to put gas in my car to get back and forth to work and school, and I purchased items for my hope chest like dishes and a sewing machine for when I would one day be out on my own. I didn't even know what a savings account was. My parents never discussed financial planning, and my only real recollection of learning about finances was my one semester of Family Planning with Ms. Streeter my senior year of high school.

When I left my first husband, and moved in with my dad and step-mom with my daughter, I quickly found a job working as an office manager for a builder, and was able to buy a used car on my own. It wasn't long and I found myself wanting more. I wanted a new car, so I went to the dealership with my grandpa and bought myself a brand new car. It was awesome; complete with a sunroof. I then was able to move out and found myself an apartment. I was so proud to be able to keep up with the expenses, and before I knew it I was filling out applications for a home loan. My dad and grandpa gave me some land, and I was able to get the loan to build a small ranch house on it. It was perfect.

By this time, I had met Jim, and we got married in the spring, moved into our new home in the summer, and had our first baby together in the fall. Life was good. But with the new home came new expenses, and as our family grew, our finances grew. I was 5 months pregnant with my third daughter when, on my way to work one morning, I was in a bad car accident. I was fine and so was our baby, but the car was totaled. The insurance company's payout did not cover the total amount owed on my car loan, as I had wrapped what I owed on my first used car into that loan. So, now here I sat with a job 30 minutes away from home, no car, and yet another car loan not paid off. I found another new car at a dealership and quickly bought that without much thought going into it. It was a beautiful black Pontiac Grand Am, and although it did have 4 doors, it was not very practical for a growing family with three small children, two still in car seats. Cars seemed to be a curse with us through those years. We traded that in for a used van, which I then traded for a car that I could deliver newspapers with during my working from home days trying to work my early MLM companies. We were struggling financially, I had car loans way over what our vehicles were worth, but we had property! This is when things really got bad. Yes, we had made some bad decisions regarding car loans, but now we were about to make the biggest financial mistake of our lives. We talked to a mortgage company and found that our house was worth a lot more money than what we owed, due to the principal we had from owning the land. Let's just refinance the house! That's a great idea. We can build an addition onto our small ranch to accommodate our growing family, and have a little extra to get that motorcycle Jim had always wanted. No. That was a terrible idea....

It didn't take long for the financial stress to start taking a toll on our marriage. Jim had already had one affair at this time. I swear my head went right out the window when I thought buying a motorcycle for myself would be a great idea. It would bring us closer together, give us common ground. Something we could do together. The kids were all in school, although Adam was only in preschool, it still allowed me some time to get a job outside of the home and still work on my MLM. So, with the extra income I was bringing in, instead of working on old debt, I went out and bought myself a Harley Davidson. Oh my goodness, was she pretty. And I loved riding. In fact, over the next couple of years, I rode more than Jim did. Now, I may be slow at figuring this whole financial thing out, but I wasn't completely stupid, and I knew what I had to do. So, with my stomach in knots I went to the bank and sat down with the loan manager. I explained that I could not afford to do this anymore, and agreed to a voluntary repossession on my car and my motorcycle. One of my saddest days ever was watching my friend who owned a towing company come pick up my vehicles. I felt like such a failure. My marriage was in complete shambles. The motorcycle had not brought us closer together, we were farther apart than ever. Luckily I had a girlfriend who sold me her car for only $500, so that I could get back and forth to work. That was in 1999, and I haven't bought a new car since. I've learned that life isn't about things, and that financial stress is one of the worse kinds of stress. Would I like a new car without rust and paint chips? Yes. Is it a priority in my life? No. Someday I will save up enough money to buy a newer used car, but payments on a brand new, high priced vehicle is not on my priority list.

And what about the house you ask? Well, that mortgage lender talked us right into taking out as much money as we could with this great low interest rate. I even called her before we signed the papers, saying I wasn't comfortable with the large payments. She assured me that she had gone over our financial statements and that we were going to be just fine. We weren't fine. At one point we even moved in with my dad, and put our house up for sale. Finances got better for a little bit, and we moved back into the house when it didn't sell. We struggled to keep our head above water. I battled with collection agencies and utility companies with their shut off notices. Life was so unOola.

We went almost a year with no paycheck from Jim after his doctors told him he had to quit working, before his disability checks started coming in. It was during this time that he had his first heart attack. And it wasn't until after Jim passed away that I realized the true mistake we had made on our mortgage. Three months after he passed, I got a letter from the mortgage company saying our payments would increase to $3,000 a month due to the adjusted interest rate on our mortgage. Seriously? How on earth was I going to be able to afford that? We went over my options, which I quickly found were slim. 1.) I could pay the new amount. 2.) I could refinance, but I hadn't worked out of the home in 4 years, so no company would give me a loan until I was back into a job for at least a year. Or 3.) Declare bankruptcy. The decision was brutal; after all, I had built this home on land that my dad had given me that had been in our family for now 5 generations. Thankfully, I had received money from Jim's funeral and Social Security to cover expenses to get me through a few months. It was during these very dark times that I saw that God always has a plan. And Jeremiah 29:11 was once again my daily go to verse.

I ended up filing for bankruptcy, and turning my home over to the bank just before Kenny and I got married. We live in a nice home on a beautiful piece of property. The home is older and someday we may find ourselves building or buying somewhere else, but for now we are concentrating on our Oola Finance. We have cars and

motorcycles that are paid off, and our house will be paid off in about 5 years. We have transportation and are warm and dry. We don't have creditors calling and leaving nasty messages, and I don't worry about how I'm going to afford dinner tonight. Our

blessings are many, and I'm so grateful to God for the journey that I've been on that helps me to appreciate the small things in life are really the big things.

We've spent a lot of time looking into Dave Ramsey's *Financial Peace University*. I think this should be a mandatory course in high school. Kids need to realize that *"If you live like no one else now, you can live like no one else later"* in life. You don't have to be enslaved to debt, and work 40 hours a week for 50 weeks a year, for 60 years. There's a better

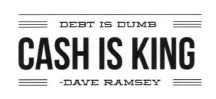

way, and that is very Oola. Start learning to pay off debt aggressively and saving for your future. There's even an oil for that! Two of my favorites are Abundance, and Oola Finance. I like to put a drop of Oola Finance in my hand, close my eyes, cup my hands around my nose and mouth and repeat, "I am financially free and living abundantly". In fact, there is a blend of oils for each of the 7 F's of Oola, along with affirmation verses that you can meditate on.

I think that this F of Oola is the hardest, because it generally takes the longest to get into balance, unless of course you have an orchard of Money Trees in your backyard. It's best to create an Oola Plan and then chart your Oola Path on how you're going to get there. Dave and Troy have made this easier by providing downloads on their website at www.Oolalife.com. I also recommend getting one of Dave Ramsey's many books and looking at his financial system of paying-off debt. If you'd like more help, and are interested in the oil blends, you can always go to my website at www.HisDropsofHope.com and check out the Infused 7 Collection.

Chapter 8 - Fun

Fun! This should be fun, right? I wish I could tell you that my Oola Journey has been filled with all kinds of fun, but in reality, I don't even think I really know what fun is. Now, I'll admit that since marrying Kenny, I have had more fun in my life than ever before, but with taking over and remodeling the pawn shop, time together to have fun outside the shop has been minimal.

So, what have I done in the past that was fun.... I love horses, and motorcycles. I've also discovered that I love bicycling and zip-lining! And pretty much anything crafty. I do enjoy papercrafting, beading and sewing. But what do I dislike more? Being alone. Yikes... I'm sure this comes from those latchkey days of going home straight from school and sitting in a quiet house until the parents got home. It's such a fine line. While I don't like being home alone, I could go days without leaving the house or seeing others. Lucky for me my life does not permit it right now. I have a fear that as I get older, I'll be a hermit. This sounds so strange as I'm rereading my words... "I don't like being alone, but yet I could be alone for days" Make up your mind, child! This is when my OolaFun gets out of balance.

I think it's quite obvious I need more fun, and obviously my Oola Journey will not be complete until the Lord calls me home. But for now I'm learning to enjoy life and to enjoy me. Kenny has taught me so many things.

He was a bachelor for about 12 years before we got married, so he had lots of time to go do fun things. He has traveled the US and Mexico with friends and by himself. He doesn't mind grabbing his snowboard and heading to a ski hill by himself, he actually enjoys the tranquility of it all.

You need to find something you're passionate about. So passionate that it doesn't matter if you're by yourself or with someone, you just want to go do it. When it comes to fun, I'm a follower. If someone is going to go do something fun, I'll go along. But if I'm by myself and the opportunity arises to do something fun, like the sun is shining and it's a beautiful day for a walk, I will sit in the house doing nothing rather than going out to do something fun. Why? Because I'm not passionate about walking outside. I do enjoy it, especially in Mid-Michigan during the fall with all of the beautiful colors and the sun dancing off the leaves, but that dreaded Oola Blocker called laziness sets in. Ugh!!! I know that if I went out there for even - 15 minutes my countenance would go up.... Excuse me, I'll be right back!

Wow! I was right, that felt so good!!! And you know what? It was fun, cause when I walked outside, Izzy (our German Shepherd) grabbed her favorite "F" word.... FRISBEE, and we played together. So, in knowing and actually proving that it is more fun to go outside then to sit and look at it through a window, what keeps me from doing more fun things? Those darn Oola Blockers like laziness, fear, self-sabotage and lack of focus, that's what. This is when I need to really focus on Oola Accelerators like passion as I discussed earlier. Love, like the love of Izzy and playing with her. Discipline! No excuses.... Just get out there and make myself have some FUN!

So, whether you are snorkeling off the coast of Croatia, zip-lining with your 82 year old mother-in-law, playing frisbee with your dog, or beating your husband at a good game of cribbage; make sure to keep the Fun in your Oola balanced with your other F's. Don't let days become weeks that become months that turn into years without fun.

My amazing
mother-in-law and I;
zip-lining during a
Lutheran women's
conference!

Kenny and I love to ride our
motorcycles. Our favorite trip was a
week through northern Michigan!

So, whether you're doing an
extreme sport, traveling or sitting
and watching a beautiful sunset…
make sure to get your OolaFun in
balance

Chapter 9 - Fitness

Fitness. To me, this is the most important F of Oola. And the most broad, because when we talk about Oola Fitness we aren't just talking about exercising. We are talking about our mind, body and soul.

Let's first start with exercise. I've always been active. In high school I played volleyball, softball, golf, cheerleading, and on the weekends we would go up north to our cabin, and I would waterski during the summer and cross-country ski during the winter. As an adult, I quit exercising when my children were younger, but when Kenny and I started dating I was in awe of his thirst to stay active. He taught me how to downhill ski, and got me back on a bicycle again. However, riding a bike was not as fun as it used to be when I was in high school. Years of not taking care of my body were evident in the sore joints I had after a short ride. While I admired his ability to ride 20 miles on a whim, my body would just simply not

let me, until about 4 years ago when I started using essential oils and educating myself on my personal wellness; what toxins are in the daily products we use and how they can affect us. Since then, my life has been dramatically changed and I'm learning to enjoy life to the fullest. I am healthier now than I have been in 30 years. I have ridden 67 miles on my bicycle in 5 hours, and I ran my first 5K... not too shabby for 50 years old.

Not only do we have to take care of our bodies and exercise, we also have to take care of what we put on and in our body. I used to be so naive about the products I used and the food I ate. I relied on the FDA to keep us safe. I mean they wouldn't knowingly let something be sold to us that would cause harm, would they? I have always known that there is big money in pharmaceuticals and our health care system. What I didn't know is how closely linked they are to the FDA, that might cause some to turn a blind eye to the wellness of the American public. It's so sad that in Europe there are over 1,300 chemicals that they have banned from being used in their make-up. In the United States there are only 11 chemicals banned from our make-up. Many of these chemicals cause cancer, infertility and have hormonal disrupters. When shopping for groceries, stick to the outside aisles of the store. Choose fresh fruits, vegetables and meats. Stay away from the inside aisles with all of the processed foods filled with preservatives. And what about our cleaning products??? Did you know that if a product bears the skull and crossbones logo that it means that 50% or more of the animals that it was tested on have died? Go check out your cupboards -now... and we wonder why we have more cases of asthma, fibromyalgia, MS and other silent illnesses now more than ever before. I am pleading with you to take control of your wellness. If you only work on one F of your Oola life, please look deeply into your environment and what you are exposing yourself to. If you'd like to discuss breaking free of the toxins in your home, I would love to help you with that. Take baby steps. It doesn't mean that you have to immediately get rid of every- yuck in your house. Maybe switch one product a week. There is a wonderful app called "Think Dirty". You can use it to scan the products in your home to see how toxic they are. They will rate the product 0-10, and show you how dirty it is in three categories; Carcinogenicity, Developmental & Reproductive toxicity and Allergies & Immunotoxicities. If a product scored a 7 or higher, it will give you their recommended healthier choices. You can start today towards your Oola life by downloading this free app and scanning the products in your home. I no longer have to worry about Emergency Room visits for severe asthma attacks after cleaning my bathroom. Aren't you ready to make a change today?

And finally, let's talk about our mind and soul. How's your mental health? After hearing most of my story,

I'm sure you can imagine that I've had some working out to do in my head…. For the most part I am now well adjusted and have worked through many of the evils I've encountered in my lifetime, but with all of the recent events coming to light of men using their influences to coerce women to do things that make them feel uncomfortable, I too had some more working out to do. Every night it was all over the TV, and one day while working at our pawn shop a male customer was overstepping the boundaries of one of our female customers. I snapped. Just like that. So many emotions came rushing in, along with the memories. Now, in writing this book I have been extremely cautious in what I shared. Many parts of my story include others that I love, and their stories that are not mine to share. So, while I won't share the gory details of parts of my childhood, or parts that may affect my children, I can tell you the strongest memory that rushed back to me that day was Clarence. He was really good at wearing his uniform, including his gun and billy club, and reminding me that he was a police officer, and who did I think people would believe? One afternoon I had been watching cartoons when he came home from work. He came in and found me sucking my thumb. Did I forget to mention that I was 3 or 4 years old at the time? He snatched me up and took me to the kitchen, laid my thumb on the counter and got out his knife. I was so scared. He had threatened to cut off my thumb if I didn't quit sucking it, and now he was going to really do it. No. He didn't cut off my thumb that day. But looking up at him in that uniform, with that knife, and his gun in his holster, definitely put an extreme fear into me. I think that is when I started twisting my hair. I went from thumb sucking into hair twisting. That sort of sick abuse continued until I was 7. I'll never forget the day that mom came to me and asked if I wanted her to leave him. I especially remember thinking, "Do you really have to ask me?" and "Who is the adult here??" I never saw him again. My grandma passed away when I was in my 20's; Clarence asked to see me, and I refused. Sometimes I wish that I had confronted him then. A couple of years ago I was volunteering at our local ministerial alliance, where I would go through applications with clients who needed financial assistance from the community. One day a woman came in who had lost her husband. She had the funds to pay for all of his funeral expenses except for the opening of his grave. If she didn't pay this upfront, they would not bury him after his funeral that week. I instantly thought of when Jim had passed away suddenly, and we had to come up with $8,000 before they would even set up visitation or write an obituary. I immediately agreed to help her with the couple of hundred dollars needed, and had her fill out the application. We prayed together, hugged and I handed her the check without even reading through her application. After she left, I looked down and saw the name she had written as her late husband's.... Clarence. The overflow of emotion came like a rushing flood. Granted, it wasn't my mom's second husband, the last names were off by only ONE letter, but the similarity and thought of him being buried brought to surface everything I needed to work through with the hurt that man had caused me. I took the rest of that day and cried and talked and cried some more. There are many essential oils that can help with feelings and emotions; in fact, we have a Feelings Collection that is fabulous. The smell of these little bottles of goodness can bring back memories that allow you to work through some of your hurts, habits and hang-ups. I have always said that I love watching God work in my life, and this encounter was no different. If we look back at our past, generally you will find that what you went through allowed you to get through or help someone else in your future. I've learned that when something happens or comes up, not to cry out, "Why, God, why?", but to ask, "What is it that you want me to learn from this, God?"

Whatever your past hurts are, it is so important to work through them. Talk to someone, whether it's a counselor, clergyman or a friend. Bringing things to the surface, and working through them is key though. I used to say that I was the best damn bricklayer ever! I can build a wall to protect myself faster than anyone. Kenny has taught me that keeping short accounts is best. Allow yourself a day if you need to calm down and diffuse a situation, but don't let something drag out over weeks, months or years and allow walls to form. Jesus instructs us in Matthew 5:23-24, "Therefore, if you are offering your gift at the altar and there remember that your brother or sister has something against you, leave your gift there in front of the altar. First go and be reconciled to them; then come and offer your gift." Enough said, right?

Chapter 10 - Oola Plan

After reading my story, have I encouraged you to want an Oola Life? I certainly hope so. Anyone can have a life of Oola. It doesn't matter where you've come from, or what you've come through. It's never too late to get your wings, and become that beautiful creation that God designed for you.

At Jim's funeral I saw our tattoo artist. I was devastated by Jim's passing, and asked to meet with him in a couple of days to get a memorial tattoo. Remember last chapter I said to learn from events in your past? Well, from this I learned to not ever make a drastic decision without much thought of what is going on your body and where... LOL I let him design the tattoo, and now years later, I had people asking, "What is that suppose to be?" A few months ago, as I was starting to write this book, I was with my mother-in-law and

sister-in-law at a scrapbooking weekend. I drew and colored the butterfly on the cover of this book. I loved it so much, that I decided to use it as a cover up on that tattoo. Although I loved the sentiment behind the tattoo as a memorial to Jim, it did not represent who I am, or where I am currently. I made sure to leave Jim's birth and death dates still visible through the tattoo, as I don't ever want to forget my past, but to move into my future of my new OolaLife. Living life to the fullest and balanced in the 7 key areas, allowing me to become that beautiful butterfly that God intended for me to be.

So, what's your plan? Are you ready for a life of balance? Are you ready for an OolaLife full of promise and blessings? Now's the time to go back to the OolaLife website and download the OolaPlan. Let's start planning where you want to be in 30 days. Just imagine the life you can be living in one year, if you start planning today!

Chapter 11 - OolaPath

Now you have set your goals that you want to achieve your OolaLife, but you'll need to stay focused. Remember my Jesus prayer? Those darn squirrels can really derail any great train taking you to your OolaLife, so you'll need to take action every day. Go back to the website, and now you can download the OolaPath worksheets. These will help you stay on track.

Know what works for you. Are you a visual person like I am? Then get a good planner and write your goals and how you're going to obtain them so that you look at them everyday. I like to put them on my bathroom mirror, write them on my chalkboard in my office, and even create framed artwork to hang on my walls.

Maybe share this book with a friend, and the two of you commit to helping each other obtain your OolaLife together, and become accountability partners! Whatever works for you, go for it! Don't wait.... Start your OolaLife today!

I like the 3 steps a day rule. Each day write down 3 things that you can do that will get you closer to your Oola Goal.

Chapter 12 - Thank you

And there we have it… my OolaLife summed up in a small, easy to read book. Of course there is more to my story, but you didn't need every little nugget of detail to know that it can be done. I truly appreciate you taking time to read this. Did you find comfort in my words? Did it encourage you to make a change? Are you inspired to write your OolaJourney and allow it to help others? How cool would it be to have a series of books of OolaJourneys???

I've created a facebook page, "OolaJourney". Join me there, and share your story. Let others know how this book helped you to make that first step in your OolaLife. Don't forget to pick up your copy of *"Oola, Find Balance in an Unbalanced World"* and get all of the information straight from the OolaGuru and the OolaSeeker. Stop by their facebook page at OolaLife and let them know that you're ready to make a change. Together we can make a difference in the world by sharing this one word… Oola.

Every day of my life I have choices. It's not always easy. Some days are tougher than others. But I strive to push through the hard days. Praying for strength, wisdom and God's will for my life.

Start each day being grateful for everything you have. Everything you've been through. Everything you've done. Make the choices that get you closer to your Oola Life, and before you know it, you'll be there!

References

To purchase *"Oola, Find Balance in an Unbalanced World"* or *"Oola for Women"* or to just learn more about Oola go to www.oolalife.com

Go to www.justiceforlily.com to see how you can help raise awareness of child abuse.

To find out more about Monique McLean's 21 Days of Prayer for your Business, go to www.lovethemcleans.com

Check out all of the reference material for finances by Dave Ramsey at www.DaveRamsey.com

You can learn more about essential oils at www.HisDropsofHope.com

Go to www.christianrecovery.com to find a recovery meeting near you.

Devotions:
> The Love Dare 354 day Couple Devotion
> Portals of Prayer by Concordia Publishing House
> Our Daily Bread by www.ourdailybread.org

Christian Radio:
> Family Life Radio
> Smile FM
> K-Love

TV/Movies:
> PureFlix